To have a child
is to be given
the world to hold
in your hands...

And the entire
universe
to try to fit
inside your heart.

— Laurel Atherton

Blue Mountain Arts®

Bestselling Books

By Susan Polis Schutz:
To My Daughter, with Love, on the Important Things in Life
To My Son, with Love
I Love You

100 Things to Always Remember... and One Thing to Never Forget
by Alin Austin

Is It Time to Make a Change?
by Deanna Beisser

Trust in Yourself
by Donna Fargo

To the One Person I Consider to Be My Soul Mate
by D. Pagels

For You, Just Because You're Very Special to Me
by Collin McCarty

Chasing Away the Clouds
by Douglas Pagels

Anthologies:
42 Gifts I'd Like to Give to You
Always Believe in Yourself and Your Dreams
Creeds of Life, Love, & Inspiration
Follow Your Dreams Wherever They Lead You
For You, My Daughter
Friends Are Forever
Friends for Life
I Love You, Mom
I'm Glad You Are My Sister
The Language of Recovery ...and Living Life One Day at a Time
Life Can Be Hard Sometimes ...but It's Going to Be Okay
Marriage Is a Promise of Love
May You Always Have an Angel by Your Side
Mottos to Live By
Take Each Day One Step at a Time
Teaching and Learning Are Lifelong Journeys
There Is Greatness Within You, My Son
These Are the Gifts I'd Like to Give to You
Think Positive Thoughts Every Day
Thoughts of Friendship
Thoughts to Share with a Wonderful Teenager
To My Child
True Friends Always Remain in Each Other's Heart
With God by Your Side ...You Never Have to Be Alone
Words of Love
You're Just like a Sister to Me

The Joys and Challenges of Motherhood

Special Edition

A collection of poems

Edited by Patricia Wayant

Blue Mountain Press™

SPS Studios, Inc., Boulder, Colorado

The publisher wishes to thank Susan Polis Schutz for permission to reprint the following poems that appear in this publication: "Today I woke up feeling strange...": Copyright © 1976 by Continental Publications. "How to Raise Children" and "An ideal mother should be...": Copyright © 1980, 1984 by Stephen Schutz and Susan Polis Schutz. All rights reserved.

Library of Congress Catalog Card Number: 99-16858
ISBN: 0-88396-525-9

ACKNOWLEDGMENTS appear on page 64.

Certain trademarks are used under license.

Manufactured in China
Third printing in hardcover: September 2002

♻ This book is printed on recycled paper.

This book is printed on fine quality, laid embossed, 80 lb. paper. This paper has been specially produced to be acid free (neutral pH) and contains no groundwood or unbleached pulp. It conforms with all the requirements of the American National Standards Institute, Inc., so as to ensure that this book will last and be enjoyed by future generations.

Library of Congress Cataloging-in-Publication Data

The joys and challenges of motherhood / edited by Patricia Wayant.
      p.   cm.
   ISBN 0-88396-525-9 (alk. paper)
   1. Motherhood Poetry. 2. American poetry—20th century. 3. Mother and child Poetry. 4. Mothers Poetry.
  I. Wayant, Patricia, 1953–
  PS595.M64J69 1999
  811'.50803520431—dc21   99-16858
                                        CIP

SPS Studios, Inc.
P.O. Box 4549, Boulder, Colorado 80306

Contents

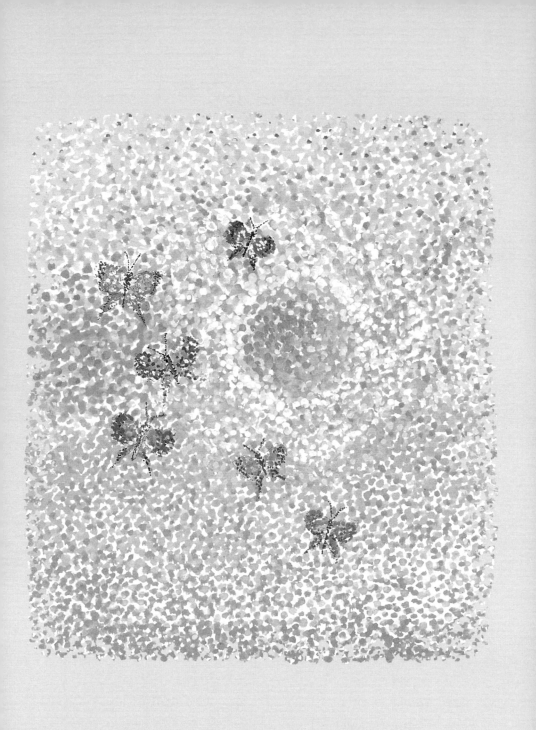

The Joys and Challenges of Motherhood

A mother is a teacher —
helping her children to learn about life,
pointing them in the right direction,
letting them make their own mistakes
and then helping them pick up
  the pieces afterwards.
A mother is a friend —
listening to her children when they need to talk,
making them talk when they don't know
  they need to,
supporting them when they are down,
and helping them to see that things
  aren't all that bad.
A mother is a role model —
leading her children by her example.
But most of all, a mother
loves unconditionally
no matter what her children do or say,
letting them know that they are not alone
  and never will be,
for they will always have a home.

— Deborah A. Brideau

A Lifetime of Happiness Begins When You Become a Mother

Nothing can quite compare
    to the joy of being a mother.
No words can describe
    the happiness
        that having a baby brings
or come close to expressing
    the pride and love you feel
        the moment you first hold
            your child in your arms.
Being a mother is a special gift
    that fills your life
        with happiness, love,
            and a lifetime of memories.

— Deanne Laura Gilbert

As a Mother...

As a mother, you may
   put yourself second sometimes —
but you will always be first
   in the eyes of your child.
You gave life,
but you will keep on giving
love, support, and wisdom.
No gifts are more priceless
   than these.
Even though being a mother
will never be easy,
remember that it is
the most important job in the world.
Trust your own judgment,
and you will do just fine.
Ask for help when you need it,
take time out for laughter
   and tears,
and trust that experience
will ease some of your fears.
As a mother,
you are shaping the future.

— Jacqueline Schiff

Becoming a Mother
Changes You

Motherhood is an experience
that opens your eyes and your heart
to exactly how magnificent
    and amazing the gift of life is.

When you become a mother,
it is amazing how your feelings,
viewpoints, goals,
and priorities change.
With one look into
your little baby's eyes,
you understand what things
are truly important in this life.

— Donna Newman

Today I woke up
feeling strange
but special
For the first time
in my life
I thought about the fact that I
could produce a baby
Out of me
from he
a little baby
Unbelievable

Sure all my friends
have had babies
but I never thought of myself
as a man's wife
or a child's mother
I am just me, leading
my own life
and in love with he

But today, I pictured
a child building sand castles
and it belonged to us

— Susan Polis Schutz

When you're a new mother,
you wake up just to watch
that tiny person who's so new
and fresh to this world
as they sleep.
You hush everything in the house
just to hear the quiet sound
of their breathing.
You give anything and everything
to protect them.
You are full of hope and joy,
fear and frustration.
Your mind may race with
a thousand questions...
"Will I be good enough?
Can I love enough?
Am I strong enough?"
You are.
You have a lifetime
of learning to share
and a tremendous amount
of love to give.
You'll be great.
All those qualities
that make you a good person
will make you an even better parent.

— Julia Escobar

Motherhood Is a Life of Commitment and Fulfillment

As a child grows, a mother does, too.
She discovers that motherhood is not the
whole of who she is, but it is an integral
part. She will never be who she was
before her child was born, and she
wouldn't want to be.
She learns that love requires not only hugs
and smiles, but also firmness and
discipline. It means saying "no" and
keeping to it, even though a part of her
always longs to say "yes."
She learns that this little being who is part
of her is also separate from her, as well.
A daughter has a will of her own. A son
can say "no" as firmly as his mother
can — and mean it!
And through the ebb and flow of life, as
years pass by, both parent and child
draw near and pull away, laugh and
cry, remember and dream.
Motherhood is a willing sacrifice, a
fulfillment, a never-ending task, and a
limitless love.

— Pamela Koehlinger

Your children are not your children.

They are the sons and daughters of Life's longing for itself.

They come through you but not from you,

And though they are with you yet they belong not to you.

You may give them your love but not your thoughts,

For they have their own thoughts.

You may house their bodies but not their souls,

For their souls dwell in the house of tomorrow, which you cannot visit, not even in your dreams.

You may strive to be like them, but seek not to make them like you.

For life goes not backward nor tarries with yesterday.

— Kahlil Gibran

What Is a Child?

A child is a touch
that bonds you for life
a smile
that makes your heart soar

A child is pride
and hope

A child is someone
whose happiness
becomes yours
and whose pain
is harder to take
than your own

A child is
laughter
that lights up your life
tears
that break your heart

A child is love that goes so deep
it becomes part of your soul

— Barbara Cage

The New Mother's Motto

"Teach me well, my little one...
To cherish the moments I have with you,
for all too soon
  they will swiftly pass away.

Remind me to pause and touch
  your soft, small cheek,
to marvel at the innocence in your eyes
and the perfect beauty of your face.

Show me how to treasure more the miracle
  that life has given me in you,
to complain less about and praise more
the boundless things you're sure to do.

In the stillness of the night,
when you wake me from my slumber,
help me to realize how truly blessed I am
to be able to hold you next to my breast,
to comfort and cradle you close to my heart.

And as the seasons pass away,
may I never look back in regret
  at what may have been.
May I instead leave a legacy
  for you to follow
as you in turn will one day welcome
  a little one of your own."

— Linda E. Knight

Some Advice to a New Mother
(from a Baby's Viewpoint)

"Our first year together
   will be fleeting.
There will be moments
that become memories
to cherish in our minds,
   our hearts,
and our scrapbooks.
We will grasp at images
and hold them for only wisps of time.

I'll change so quickly.
You'll grow as much as I do,
   and in as many ways.
The trying, crying times
   are but moments, too.
They will pass and, in passing,
will make memories that are
as wonderful to hold as I am now.

Trust yourself, for God chose you
   to be my mother,
knowing that you will love me,
   care for me,
      and know me
as no one else ever will."

— Linda Ferree

The love between a mother
and her child
is a bond of the strongest kind.
It is a love of the present,
interwoven with memories
of the past
and dreams of the future.
It is strengthened by overcoming obstacles
and facing fears and challenges together.
It is having pride in each other
and knowing that your love
can withstand anything.
It is sacrifice and tears,
laughter and hugs.
It is understanding, patience,
and believing in each other.
It is wanting only the best
for each other
and wanting to help any time
there is a need.
It is respect, a hug,
and unexpected kindness.
It is making time to be together
and knowing just what to do and say.
It is an unconditional,
forever kind of love.

— Barbara Cage

I can still recall the day my son was born. I can picture his innocent and gorgeous face. I knew in an instant that I would be falling for that face the rest of my life.

He had so much grace about him. As I got to know him and love him, it wasn't long before I knew the beauty that was also deep in his heart.

From a very young age, he was thoughtful and caring. His kindness surfaced over the years on a daily basis. Every day since his birth, I have felt so blessed.

I have learned many lessons from him. He was very forgiving of others and always patient, looking to do things a better way if he couldn't get it done the first time.

His laughter was plentiful and so delightful. Even after a hard day at work, hearing it could make my troubles melt away.

He is a ray of sunshine, and I know the world is a better place because he is in it.

— Betsy Bertram

The first time I held my daughter
was a magical moment.
I remember the first time she smiled;
I still carry that memory with me.
The times I cuddled her
were cradled with tenderness.
Often and silently,
she spoke love to me with her eyes.

I wouldn't trade the countless
fingerprints she left behind
for a dozen unmarked walls.
And all the times her curiosity
led her to my closets and cupboards,
and her imagination left its mark,
only made me love her more.
I loved her giggles then,
and I love them now.

I've seen her in deep thought,
and I've seen her acting silly.
I've captured her moods and our memories
and sewn them into my heart.

When she came along,
I knew she would change my world,
but what I didn't know then
was that I would also gain
a lifelong friend.

— Kathryn Leibovich

Being a mother is wanting
to pick up your children each time
they fall,
but teaching them to
pick up themselves instead.

Being a mother is wanting
to keep your children from all hurt and harm,
but knowing that they must be
taught to take care of themselves.

Being a mother is wanting
to give your children the best of everything,
but knowing they will
value life more if they wait
and work for many of their rewards.

Being a mother is wanting
to love your children with every aspect
    of yourself,
but knowing that some of
    the best love is given
quietly, secretly,
and in ways that they can
understand.

— Karen Kolpien—Bugaj

If anyone ever told
a woman pondering motherhood
how many dishes she would wash,
how many diapers she would change,
or how many spelling words
she would relearn,
she'd probably think twice
before having a child.

If anyone were to mention that the
terrible two's aren't half as
demanding as the turbulent teens,
that school and sports activities
require a mother's lifetime commitment,
and that friends, phones, and malls
are the essence of a young one's desires,
she might have a second thought
or two.

But the funny thing about motherhood
is that once you are a mother,
you can never imagine your life
without the love and joy of your child.
Because with each and every obligation
and the endless amount of responsibility,
there is a wonderful feeling of happiness
that enters your heart
and stays with you wherever you go.

It is the feeling of LOVE...
the most beautiful emotion in life.

— Deanna Beisser

Sometimes, looking deep into the eyes of a child, you are conscious of meeting a glance full of wisdom. The child has known nothing yet but love and beauty — all this piled-up world knowledge you have acquired is unguessed at by him. And yet you meet this wonderful look that tells you in a moment more than all the years of experience have seemed to teach.

— Hildegarde Hawthorne

Women know
The way to rear up children (to be just)
They know a simple, merry, tender knack
Of tying sashes, fitting baby-shoes,
And stringing pretty words that make no sense,
And kissing full sense into empty words.

— Elizabeth Barrett Browning

A Very Special Love

Between a mother and child,
there is a special love
that exists nowhere else.
A mother is someone who loves
and is never afraid to show that love.
A mother sometimes pushes aside
  her own needs
to focus on the needs of others.
A mother is a haven of love,
    a listening ear when no one else cares
        or has time to listen.
A mother makes time.
A mother gives advice when asked
but always with the understanding
that it is only advice,
leaving her child free
to make his or her own choices.
Though there are some times
when mother and child don't agree,
a mother respects her child's choices,
encourages her child's decisions,
and listens to her child's reasoning.
A mother is all these things
to her child, and more.

— Dale Harcombe

A mother's love is... especially unique because it is ever-trustful, ever-devoted, ever-forgiving, ever-tender, ever-unchanging, ever-enduring.

— Samuel Johnson

Mighty is the force of motherhood!

— George Eliot

Children are the anchors that hold a mother to life.

— Sophocles

There is nothing,
no power, no feeling,
that can match that
of gazing into the eyes
of a child —
a creation of love and respect
between two people.

— Tracey Smerdon

God could not
be everywhere,
so he created
mothers.

— Jewish Proverb

The hand that rocks the cradle
Is the hand that rules the world.

— William Ross Wallace

How to Raise Children

Children learn from their parents
Set the example
that you want them to follow
Treat your children kindly
and they will be kind
Treat your children gently
and they will be gentle
Show your children truth
and they will be truthful
Show your children goodness
and they will be good
Show your children thoughtfulness
and they will be thoughtful
Show your children strength
and they will be strong
Show your children courage
and they will be courageous
Show your children beauty
and they will be beautiful
Show your children freedom
and they will be free
Encourage your children's creativity
and they will be creative
Encourage your children's sensitivity
and they will be sensitive
Treat your children special
and they will be special
Children learn from their parents
Show your children love
every minute of every day
and they will show love back

— Susan Polis Schutz

As a Mother,
You'll Always Want
to Be There for Your Children

When they are little, they need you all the time — to feed them, wash them, and lay them down to sleep. But as they grow, all of that changes. They need more freedom, the chance to prove to you — and more importantly, to themselves — that they are grown up.

As a parent, the hardest thing you ever have to do is give your children the space to express who they are. It is difficult to sit by and watch them make decisions you know are unwise, yet not be able to offer your advice. You hate to see them upset or disappointed in themselves, and your first reaction will be to hold them in your arms and comfort them. But they probably won't let you. They will be determined to do things their way, and maybe you can understand that because you were young once, too.

When you are a parent, everything seems different somehow. You want to protect your child, no matter what, to shield them from an often cruel world where wishes don't always come true and hearts can be broken. Seeing your child full of hurt is the toughest part of parenting, but it's also reality.

All you can do is be there for them if and when they ever need you. Even when they're adults, they'll still be the baby you once rocked in your arms, and that feeling — that maternal instinct — will never subside. You will always want to take care of them, comfort them, listen to their fears, and encourage their dreams. For you're a mother, and that's what mothers do.

— T. L. Nash

It Takes
Someone Special
to Be a Mother

It takes a positive attitude
to remain optimistic
when the going gets rough.
It takes a lot of self-confidence
to stand strong
when it would be so much easier
just to give in.
It takes belief in yourself
and your family
to find the power to work
toward a better day.
It takes tenderness of spirit
and gentleness of heart
to respond to life's
day-to-day changes,
with your total concentration
focused on one thing:
the health and well-being
of your family.
It takes a woman who has
a unique way of transforming
life's difficult moments
into love's greatest memories.

— Linda E. Knight

A Mother's Résumé

I can hear a child's footsteps and determine
  a 102-degree temperature,
While sound asleep and several rooms away.
I can officially score a Little League game
And fit in a carpool pick-up during the Seventh
  Inning Stretch.

I can juggle a nursing baby in one arm,
While cooking a five-course meal with the other.
I can match the correct laundry with the exact
  family member,
Not losing even one sock or shrinking one shirt.

I can read a Dr. Seuss book with one hand,
While winning at jacks with the other.
I can organize 150 women with limited time
  and culinary talent
Into the largest bake sale our school has ever seen.

I can pretend interest in a discussion of taxes
  with my husband,
While planning a PTA fund-raiser in my head.
I can counsel a pre-teenage girl in the throes of
  her first love
Without sounding like my mother.

I can fix a garbage disposal with a broom handle
While saving our cat from a sibling tug-of-war.
I can still fit into the dress I bought for my first job
And truly be thankful that the retro look is deemed
   fashionable.

I can be the perfect smiling hostess and corporate wife
While long-winded clients dissect marketing plans
   and spreadsheets.
I can wallpaper the master bedroom
And watch my son play high-school football
   without screaming or fainting.

Perhaps these talents do not overly impress
Or fit succinctly on a résumé,
But surely they must count as classes passed,
And will help me get a "real-life" job someday.

— Susan Norton

Raising Children Isn't Always Easy

Sometimes it's hard
to be a parent —
especially when you look
at that young person
(the one with the scowl
    and bad attitude)
and you wonder how it
could possibly be your child.
There are times when you
may look at your child and wonder...
Is this the same person who
clutched your finger so tightly
the day they were born,
or who used to look up to you
and think you were
the absolute best?
You wonder when the two of you
grew so far apart,
or where the respect
and friendship
got pushed aside and buried.
You cling to memories
and hold that child
close to your heart,
while you hope and pray
you make it through
one day at a time.
And you will.

Even though it isn't always obvious,
the bond of love never breaks
between a parent and a child.
It gets stretched to the limits,
and it may need constant
mending and repair.
But in the end, you'll both
be proud of its strength
and grateful for its endurance.
Until then, remember that
the only thing harder
than being a parent...
is being a child.

— Barbara Cage

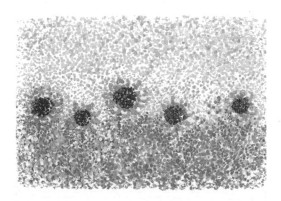

"The House Didn't Get Cleaned Today"

A poem to remind you why that's okay

The last time someone asked me what I've been up to, I didn't know what to say ➤ The house didn't get cleaned today ➤ My career didn't advance ➤ My life didn't get any more organized than it was before ➤ My "to-do" list didn't begin to get done; it might have even grown by an inch or two! ➤ I didn't live up to my horoscope's prediction for the day ➤ I didn't even have time to remember which bills needed to be paid ➤ I barely managed to grab a bite of lunch, let alone wonder how to transform macaroni into the "evening entrée" ➤ The last time I looked, I don't think my waistline had gotten much smaller, but I'm pretty sure the bank balance has ➤ I'm not driving the latest car, or living in my dream house, or doing lots of other things some people think are essential to do ➤ But I am doing something that's the most important thing in the entire world to me...

I'm cherishing the moments, I'm trying to meet the challenges, and I'm doing my part to raise a very precious family.

— Laurel Atherton

What It Means
to Be a Mother

To be a mother is not just
To create life,
But to nurture and shape it.
It is to instill in your child
A sense of absolute security
And self-worth;
To envelop your child
In a protective shield of
Unconditional love.

To be a mother is to have
Within your power to give
An indescribable sense of comfort
That can be found nowhere in the world
But in your eyes, your arms,
And your words.

It is to plant a garden of knowledge
And virtues,
While always weeding out
The external intruders
Of ignorance and prejudice.

It is to be able to look
At your child
At any stage of life
And feel proud of the person
They've become.

— Lynn Barnhart

Every Child

Every child should know a hill,
And the clean joy of running down its long slope
With the wind in his hair.
He should know a tree —
The comfort of its cool lap of shade,
And the supple strength of its arms
Balancing him between earth and sky
So he is the creature of both.
He should know bits of singing water —
The strange mysteries of its depths,
And the long sweet grasses that border it.
Every child should know some scrap
Of uninterrupted sky, to shout against;
And have one star, dependable and bright,
For wishing on.

— Edna Casler Joll

Children Create
the Best Memories

When the years behind you are many
and your hair is white like snow,
the happiest days of your life
will be the ones that echo
with the laughter of children.

Long after your children are grown
    and gone, you will remember...
the pride of counting fingers and toes,
the soft scent of a freshly bathed baby,
those first wobbly steps,
the thrill of their first word,
swinging in the spring sunshine,
dancing in the leaves of autumn,
bundling up for Old Man Winter,
and the magic of Christmas morning
    as seen through the eyes of a child.

Long after the dirty dishes are forgotten,
along with the early morning feedings
    and the dread of chicken pox,
the echo of laughter will remain.
The remnants of hearing a child laugh with glee
will return those special, wondrous,
    child–filled memories —
like that magical, peaceful feeling of love
    you only get when watching
the child you love fast asleep.

— Beth Fagan Quinn

The Miracle of Life

Life is precious
We hear it so often
it becomes
a litany without meaning
until the moment when
life explodes upon you
Pain and ecstasy at once
place within your arms that perfect
precious entity
The absolute realization of an idea
that words keep in the shadow
of our consciousness
A kind universe
The smiling face of God
Good beyond measure
This tiny individual —
this proof of hope and truth
and all things beautiful
The wonder of creation that is
your child.

— Danielle Morrison–MacNeil

44

A Mother's Promise

As a mother, I promise
that I will always try my best
to be a good parent.
I will always believe in my children
and give them the encouragement
they need to achieve their goals
and reach for their dreams.
I promise that I will offer
patience, kindness,
and understanding
when they need it.
I will try to teach them by example
the right beliefs and values.
I will listen even when
I'd rather give them my own opinions.
I will try to be not only
the best mother,
but the best friend I can possibly be.
But most of all, I promise
that I will always love them
without fail and without question.
I will love them enough
to hold them tightly
yet let them go when they need it,
to allow them the freedom
to learn and grow.
I will love them
with all my heart always.

— Deanne Laura Gilbert

45

Love Is the Most Important Lesson You Can Teach

If there could be only one thing in life to
teach your children, teach them to love...

To respect others so that they may find
respect in themselves;
To learn the value of giving, so that if ever
there comes a time in their lives when
someone is really in need, they will give;
To act in a manner that they would wish to
be treated; to be proud of themselves;
To laugh and smile as much as they can, in
order to help bring joy back into this world;
To have faith in others; to be understanding;
To stand tall in this world and to learn to
depend on themselves;
To only take from this earth those things
which they really need, so there will be
enough for others;
To not depend on money or material things
for their happiness, but
To learn to appreciate the people who love
them, the simple beauty that God gave
them, and to find peace and security
within themselves...

For all these things are love.

— Donna Dargis

MOTHERHOOD:
A Celebration of Life

It's LEARNING: You learn from your children as much as they learn from you. As you struggle to help them toward adulthood, they escort you to their wonderful place of innocence, imagination, and delight.

It's HAVING FUN: Get on the floor and play with your kids every day. Create opportunities for fun. Dirty dishes will always be there. Children grow too quickly.

It's LIMITS: Not only do you teach children limits, you learn your own limits for patience and your endurance for long, challenging days. You also learn there is one thing that _is_ limitless: your feeling of love toward your children.

It's WATCHING THEM SLEEP: At the end of each day, you recall the greatest joys and challenges — how they make you so angry and then so happy a moment later. Asleep, though, they are nothing less than angels.

It's TIME FOR YOU: Every mother learns that time for herself is essential to renew and recharge. Two hours alone to yourself when someone else is responsible for your kids can mean days of better parenting. When you feel good about yourself and are happy, everyone's better off.

It's LOVE: Snuggling together for bedtime stories or for popcorn and rented movies. Unsolicited "I love you's." Sloppy kisses and clumsy hugs. Parenting brings more love than we could ever hope for — everlasting, unconditional love of the greatest lengths and depths.

— Donna Gephart

An ideal mother should be
strong and guiding
understanding and giving
An ideal mother should be
honest and forthright
confident and able
An ideal mother should be
relaxed and soft
flexible and tolerant
But most of all
an ideal mother should be a
loving woman
who is always there when needed
and who
by being happy and satisfied
with herself
is able to be happy and loving
with her children

— Susan Polis Schutz

The Sixteen Gifts
a Mother Gives Her Children

Hope that is woven into tomorrow ‑•
Love that is sewn into the seam of each
new day ‑• Showing, by being a beautiful
example, the path to take to help you find
your way ‑• Warmth and care and
tenderness ‑• Understanding when no one
else seems to comprehend ‑• Believing so
much that you believe, too — that anything
broken can mend ‑• Dreams, hearts, and
wishful thoughts are carefully tended there ‑•
No one is better at reflecting life's goodness ‑•
A mother is a precious mirror ‑• Within the
garden of her days, children blossom and
grow ‑• Thanks to her encouragement, she
always makes sure they know ‑• The family
is a constant treasure, valued more than
any riches are worth...

What a mother gives her children...
are the sweetest gifts on this earth.

— Collin McCarty

Home Never Feels the Same After They're Gone

I wish that I could have
bottled their giggles
when they were small
and collected all of their
handprints
from each windowpane.

If I could have done this,
I would take them out gently
whenever I need to,
and spread them across everything.
Then, I would find such joy
in remembering.

But I have no giggles
or handprints
to hold or to scatter,
and remembering is somewhat bittersweet,
for home will never be
the same without
the sound of their laughter
and the gift of their presence
spilling out from every room.

— Priscilla Wright

What Is a Son?

A son is a warm spot in your heart and a smile on your lips.

In the beginning, he is charmingly innocent, putting his complete trust in you.

He comes to you for a hand to hold and for the security only your arms can provide.

He shares his tales of adventure and knows how proud you are of his discoveries and accomplishments.

All of his problems can be solved by a hug and a kiss from you, and the bond you share is so strong it is almost tangible.

Time passes, and your innocent little boy starts to test his limits. He lets go of your hand to race into the midst of life without thinking ahead or looking both ways.

His problems have grown along with him, and he has learned that you can't always make his life better or kiss his troubles away.

He spends much of his time away from you, and though you long for the closeness you once shared, he chooses independence and privacy.

Discoveries and accomplishments aren't as easy to come by now, and sometimes he wonders about his worth.

But you know the worth of that young man. He is your past and your future. He is hopes and dreams that have made it through each and every disappointment and failure.

In your heart, your son is precious and treasured. Together, you struggled through the years trying to find the right amount of independence for each new stage of his life, until finally, you had to learn to let him go.

Now you put your trust in him, leaving that son whom you hold so dear totally in his own care. You hope he always remembers that you have a hand for him to hold and arms to provide comfort or support.

Most of all, you hope that he believes in himself as much as you believe in him, and that he knows how much you love him.

— Barbara Cage

The Love Between
a Mother and Daughter

I have worn a locket since the day my daughter was born. Not the kind made of silver or gold; it's made of something much more durable than that.

My locket hangs across my heart and shines more brightly than can be imagined. If you open it up, you'll see pictures of my daughter and me, everlasting and fond memories that began the day she was born. She was so small, looking up at me with eyes so tiny and trusting. I knew from that day forward that it would be my job to ensure that her soul's reflection would always mirror trust.

Before I knew it, she was taking her first steps. Those steps soon took her to school. It filled me with joy to see her smile at me with her front teeth missing, asking endless questions about the world. I tried to answer all her questions so she'd know that they were important.

As she faced each new dawn, I relished every moment that she grew, physically and spiritually, learning new things about life and making new friends who would embrace her in days to come. I also knew that with her determined strength, someday soon she would fly.

It seemed that in the blink of an eye she was all grown up. Her steps were taking her away from the skies she used to play under in the backyard and into a bigger horizon beyond. She was beginning to find her own answers.

I know within the locket, memories will always keep my little girl close to me. The locket sparkles eternally, because it's cast from a love that never fades, the love between a mother and daughter... life's most precious gem.

— Heatherlee Anne Mace

Children Grow Up
All Too Quickly

All too quickly,
they grow out of your arms
that held them so close,
and they stand at your side,
holding on to your hand.

All too quickly,
they let go of your hand
and place their arms around
    your shoulders,
hugging you as times go by.

All too quickly,
they are standing tall and strong
    on their own,
independent and self–assured,
letting you see the person they
    have become
and knowing that you couldn't be
    more proud.

All too quickly,
the days of childhood come and go,
but the memories of those times
stay as clear in your mind as ever.
And because they are your children,
they will always be welcomed
    into your arms,
for they will never be too old or too big
to be held close to your heart.

— Deanna Beisser

The Bond Between
Mother and Child
Lasts a Lifetime

The bond between mother and child
is a special one.
It remains unchanged by time
   or distance.
It is the purest love —
unconditional and true.
It is understanding of any situation
and forgiving of any mistake.
It creates a support that is constant
while everything else changes.
It is a friendship based on
mutual love, respect,
and a genuine liking
of each other as a person.
It is knowing that no matter
where you go or who you are,
there is someone who truly loves you
and is always there
to support and console you.
When a situation seems impossible,
you make it through together
by holding on to each other.

The bond between mother and child
is strong enough to withstand
harsh words and hurt feelings,
for it is smart enough to always
see the love beyond the words.
It is brave enough to always
  speak the truth,
even when lies would be easier.
It is always there —
  anytime, anywhere —
whenever it is needed.
It is a gift held in the heart
  and in the soul,
and it cannot be taken away
or exchanged for another.
To possess this love is a treasure
that makes life more valuable.

— Stephanie Douglass

A Mother's Love
Is Forever

There is an overwhelming feeling
of love that fills a mother's heart
whenever she stops and thinks
of what a miracle her children are to her life
and how absolutely wonderful
    her life is because of them.
All parents feel a special
    kind of endless love for their children,
yet there is no way for a child ever
to comprehend the depth of that love
until the day comes
when they are parents, too.

A child is a miracle that never
ceases to be miraculous.
A child is full of beauty
and forever beautiful.
A child is loving and caring
and truly amazing.
Time will pass by,
and so many things will change,
but the absolute joy
that a child brings to life
will only grow deeper
and more important.

— Deanna Beisser

Motherhood Is the Best!

For all the tears that
   fill a mother's eyes and the
   prayers she kneels to pray;
For all the fearful, scary things
   that her laughter chases away.
For her extra–special kindness
   when a child's feelings have been bruised;
For her gentle understanding
   when her child feels most confused.
For all the work and worry
   that her children cause her to endure;
For the confidence she has in them
   when they feel most unsure.
For holding them up straight and tall
   when dreams crash around them;
For all the faith she has in them
   when others seem to doubt them.
For her gentle words that teach them
   all the things they want to know;
For the times her heart breaks
   as she stands back to watch them go.
For the empty nights she helps them through
   when they feel most alone;
For teaching them to make it through
   the nighttime on their own.
For guiding them with loving hands
   through hours and hours of tears;
For all the smiles she smiles
   just for them throughout the years.
For the pride in them that she feels
   with every step they take;
For teaching them to live with
   and learn from each mistake.
For these things that are mentioned
   and all the rest...
Motherhood is the best!

— Dianna Barnett

ACKNOWLEDGMENTS

We gratefully acknowledge the permission granted by the following authors, publishers, and authors' representatives to reprint poems or excerpts from their publications.

Julia Escobar for "When you're a new mother...." Copyright © 1999 by Julia Escobar. All rights reserved.

Pamela Koehlinger for "Motherhood Is a Life of Commitment and Fulfillment." Copyright © 1999 by Pamela Koehlinger. All rights reserved.

Alfred A. Knopf, Inc. and Gibran National Committee, P.O. Box 116-5487, Beirut, Lebanon for "Your children are not your children..." from "On Children" from THE PROPHET by Kahlil Gibran. Copyright © 1923 by Kahlil Gibran and renewed 1951 by Administrators C.T.A. of Kahlil Gibran Estate and Mary G. Gibran. All rights reserved.

Barbara Cage for "What Is a Child?" and "Raising Children Isn't Always Easy." Copyright © 1999 by Barbara Cage. All rights reserved.

Linda E. Knight for "The New Mother's Motto." Copyright © 1999 by Linda E. Knight. All rights reserved.

Betsy Bertram for "I can still recall...." Copyright © 1999 by Betsy Bertram. All rights reserved.

Deanna Beisser for "If anyone ever told...." Copyright © 1999 by Deanna Beisser. All rights reserved.

Susan Norton for "A Mother's Résumé." Copyright © 1999 by Susan Norton. All rights reserved.

T. L. Nash for "As a Mother...." Copyright © 1999 by T. L. Nash. All rights reserved.

Lynn Barnhart for "What It Means to Be a Mother." Copyright © 1999 by Lynn Barnhart. All rights reserved.

Beth Fagan Quinn for "Children Create the Best Memories." Copyright © 1999 by Beth Fagan Quinn. All rights reserved.

Danielle Morrison-MacNeil for "The Miracle of Life." Copyright © 1999 by Danielle Morrison-MacNeil. All rights reserved.

Deanne Laura Gilbert for "A Mother's Promise." Copyright © 1999 by Deanne Laura Gilbert. All rights reserved.

Donna Gephart for "MOTHERHOOD: A Celebration of Life." Copyright © 1999 by Donna Gephart. All rights reserved.

Priscilla Wright for "Home Never Feels the Same After They're Gone." Copyright © 1999 by Priscilla Wright. All rights reserved.

Heatherlee Anne Mace for "The Love Between a Mother and Daughter." Copyright © 1999 by Heatherlee Anne Mace. All rights reserved.

A careful effort has been made to trace the ownership of poems and excerpts used in this anthology in order to obtain permission to reprint copyrighted materials and give proper credit to the copyright owners. If any error or omission has occurred, it is completely inadvertent, and we would like to make corrections in future editions provided that written notification is made to the publisher:

SPS STUDIOS, INC., P.O. Box 4549, Boulder, CO 80306.